Professional Paper P7
Advanced Audit and Assurance (UK)

GW00420231

First edition 2007, Ninth edition July 2014

ISBN 9781 4727 1134 2

e ISBN 9781 4727 1190 8

British Library Cataloguing-in-Publication Data
A catalogue record for this book is available from the
British Library

Published by

BPP Learning Media Ltd,
BPP House, Aldine Place,
142-144 Uxbridge Road,
London W12 8AA

www.bpp.com/learningmedia

Printed in the UK by Ashford
Colour Press Ltd

Unit 600
Fareham Reach
Gosport
Hampshire PO13 0FW

Welcome to BPP Learning Media's ACCA **Passcards** for **P7 Advanced Audit and Assurance (UK)**.

- They focus on your exam and **save you time**.
- They incorporate **diagrams** to kick start your memory.
- They follow the overall **structure** of the BPP Learning Media's Texts, but BPP Learning Media's ACCA **Passcards** are not just a condensed book. Each card has been separately designed for clear presentation. Topics are self contained and can be grasped visually.
- ACCA **Passcards** are still **just the right size** for pockets, briefcases and bags.

Run through the **Passcards** as often as you can during your final revision period. The day before the exam, try to go through the **Passcards** again. You will then be well on your way to passing your exams.

Good luck!

Contents

1: International regulatory environments for audit and assurance

This chapter looks at the regulatory environment in which auditing takes place. Directors of companies are encouraged to follow what has been set down as good practice by various government committees.

Directors need to ensure that internal controls perform effectively, as part of their statutory duties. Recent moves have sought transparency by asking directors to report to shareholders on these issues.

International Regulatory Framework

IFAC

IAASB   IESBA

International Standards on Auditing (ISAs)

IESBA *Code of Ethics*

UK Regulatory Framework

Auditors

EU requires member states to approve auditors.

In UK **RSBs**, eg ACCA

Audit framework

The **FRC** regulates corporate reporting in the UK, and issued the UK Corporate Governance Code.

The FRC issues auditing standards, practice notes and bulletins.

Advantages

- Increased **confidence** in financial statements
- **Frees** executive directors to manage
- **Clear reporting lines** for internal audit/impartial link for external audit
- Creates **culture opposed to fraud**

Disadvantages

- **Selecting suitable** independent non-executive **directors** can be **difficult**
- **Formality** may dissuade reporting on **judgmental** issues
- **Cost** of audit committee

Liaison with external auditors

- Determine scope of external audit
- Forum to link directors/auditors
- Deal with auditors' reservations
- Obtain information for auditors

Duties

Review of internal audit

Review of internal controls

Special investigations

Codes of Best Practice for corporate governance are increasingly common worldwide. The P7 exam focuses on the guidance given in the **UK Corporate Governance Code**.

UK Corporate Goverance Code

Compliance with the UK Corporate Governance Code is **voluntary**, but all UK **listed** entities must **report** on **how they have applied it** (in the annual report).

This is known as the '**comply or explain**' basis. Listed entities must either comply with the Code, or explain why they have not done so.

Key effects on auditors

- Auditors must review compliance with code and statement of compliance/non-compliance.
- The Code requires companies to establish an audit committee.
- Listed (UK FTSE 350) companies applying the Code must put the external **audit** out to **tender** at least every **ten years**.

Directors

Internal controls and risk management are very important in fulfiling directors' duties to the shareholders, which are:

- To safeguard assets
- To prevent and detect fraud

Protect the investment of the shareholder

Therefore directors:

- **Set up** a system of **internal control**
- **Review** its **effectiveness**
- Consider the need for **internal audit**

Auditors

As part of their audit:

- Ascertain what the controls are
- Review controls
- Evaluate controls
- Determine audit approach based on controls

Can also offer services

- To review controls
- Report to shareholders as a function separate from audit

Money laundering

The process by which criminals attempt to conceal the true origin and ownership of the proceeds of their criminal activity, allowing them to maintain control over the proceeds and, ultimately, providing a legitimate cover for their sources of income.

Money laundering is the attempt to conceal the origin of 'dirty' money by making it look legitimate or 'clean'. There are 3 stages:

(1) **Placement**. This is the introduction or placement of the illegal funds into the financial system.

(2) **Layering**. This is passing the money through a large number of transactions or 'layers', so that it becomes very difficult to trace it to its original source.

(3) **Integration**. This is the final integration of funds back into the legitimate economy.

Exam focus

Exam questions in this area may require you to indentify that money laundering is taking place. This means using **professional sketicism**.

Criminal offences in the UK

- Possessing, dealing with or concealing the **proceeds** of any **crime**
- Attempting, assisting or incitement to commit money laundering
- **Failure** of an individual in the regulated sector **to report a suspicion** of money laundering
- **Tipping off**

Money Laundering Regulations 2007

- Appoint a ML Reporting officer (MLRO)
- Undertake **Customer Due Diligence**
- Reporting **suspicion** of money laundering
- Maintaining specific **records**
- Putting **internal procedures** in place to ensure continued compliance with regulations
- **Training staff** in all these issues

The **auditor's responsibilities** for considering law and regulations as part of their audit is discussed in ISA 250A:

- **Plan**
  Should plan so as to identify any examples of non-compliance

- **Evidence**
  Should obtain sufficient appropriate audit evidence of **compliance** with laws and regulations with a **direct affect** on **material accounts** and **disclosures** in the FS.

- **Document findings**
  Document non-compliance and the results of discussion with management, those charged with governance and third parties.

Management are responsible for ensuring that laws and regulations are kept.

Reporting non-compliance

Management

- Non-compliance should be discussed with those charged with governance

Shareholders

- Consider the impact on audit report – modified opinion

Third parties

- Is there a statutory duty?
- Is it in the public interest?
- Obtain legal advice

2: Code of Ethics and Conduct

Much of this chapter is revision from your previous studies. You must understand the principles-based approach and be familiar with the guidance issued by ACCA, the IESBA and the FRC.

*In the exam you are likely to be faced with **scenarios** where you have to **apply** your knowledge, identify ethical **threats** and recommend appropriate **safeguards**.*

ACCA Code of Ethics and Conduct

The Code contains a conceptual framework, setting out five fundamental principles. This recognises that it is impossible to define every single situation that may give rise to a threat, and to prescribe specific safeguards for each. The ACCA Code has been based on the IESBA *Code of Ethics for Professional Accountants*.

Integrity

To be **straightforward** and **honest** in all professional and business relationships

Objectivity

To not allow **bias, conflicts of interest** or **undue influence** of others to override professional or business judgements

Professional competence and due care

To **maintain professional knowledge** and **skill** at a level required to ensure that a client or employer receives competent professional services based on **current developments** in practice, legislation, techniques, and should **act diligently** and in accordance with applicable **technical and professional standards** when providing professional services.

Confidentiality

To respect the confidentiality of information acquired as a result of professional and business relationships and, therefore, **not disclose** any such information **to third parties** without **proper** and **specific authority**, unless there is a **legal** or **professional right** or **duty to disclose**, nor use the information for the **personal advantage** of the professional accountant or third parties.

Professional behaviour

To **comply** with relevant **laws and regulations** and to avoid any action that **discredits the profession**.

Although not a fundamental principle, auditors must plan and perform the audit with **professional skepticism**. ISA 200 defines this as follows:

Professional skepticism is an attitude that includes a questioning mind, being alert to conditions which may indicate possible misstatement, and a critical assessment of evidence.

Independence of mind

The state of mind that permits the provision of an opinion without being affected by influences that compromise professional judgement, allowing an individual to act with integrity, and exercise objectivity and professional scepticism.

Objectives of this section of the ACCA code

to help firms and members to...

Step 1 **Identify threats** to independence

Step 2 **Evaluate** the **significance** of the threats identified

Step 3 **Apply safeguards**, when necessary, to **eliminate** the **threats** or **reduce** them to an **acceptable level**

Independence in appearance

The avoidance of facts and circumstances that are so significant that a reasonable and informed third party, having knowledge of all relevant information, including safeguards applied, would reasonably conclude a firm's, or a member's, integrity, objectivity or professional scepticism had been compromised.

The FRC issues ethical standards.

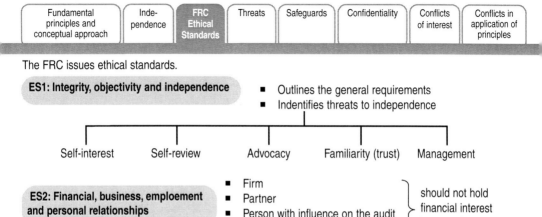

ES1: Integrity, objectivity and independence

- Outlines the general requirements
- Indentifies threats to independence

Self-interest   Self-review   Advocacy   Familiarity (trust)   Management

ES2: Financial, business, emploement and personal relationships

- Firm
- Partner
- Person with influence on the audit
- Their immediate family

} should not hold financial interest in an audit client

ES3: Long association with the audit engagment

safeguards required →

- Rotate partner
- Involving additional partner
- Independent internal quality control review

Additionally, for *listed* companies

- Change partner every 5 years
- Review safeguards if senior staff involved > 7 years

ES4: Fees, remuneration and evaluation plicies, litigation, gifts and hospitality

- No contingent fees
- Overdue fees? consider whether appropriate to continue

> 10% annual fee income [15% non-listed company] ——→ should not act as auditors

> 5% annual fee income [10% non-listed company] ——→ disclosure and implement safeguards

Accounting service

- Non acceptable for listed client, or
- Taking management role

ES5: Non-audit services provided to audit clients

Internal audit

- Generally acceptable
- *Unless* placing reliance during audit

Taxation

- Generally acceptable, unless
  - Contingent fee
  - Taking management role
  - Acting as advocate

Valuation

- Non acceptable, if subjective, and
- Material to FS

Information technology

- Not acceptable if significant to accounting system, or
- Undertaking management role

Compliance with the fundamental principles may potentially be threatened by a broad range of circumstances:

Threats

(a) **Self-interest** threat, eg financial interests, incentive compensation arrangements, undue dependence on fees

(b) **Self-review** threat, eg data being reviewed by the same person responsible for preparing it

(c) **Advocacy** threat, eg acting as an advocate on behalf of an assurance client in litigation or disputes with third parties

(d) **Familiarity** threat, eg former partner of the firm being a director or officer of the client

(e) **Intimidation** threat, eg threat of dismissal or replacement, being pressured to reduce inappropriately the extent of work performed in order to reduce fees

3 categories of safeguard exist:

- Created by profession, legislation, regulations
- Created by the individual
- In the work environment

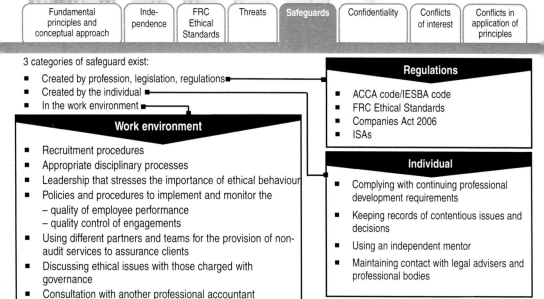

Regulations

- ACCA code/IESBA code
- FRC Ethical Standards
- Companies Act 2006
- ISAs

Work environment

- Recruitment procedures
- Appropriate disciplinary processes
- Leadership that stresses the importance of ethical behaviour
- Policies and procedures to implement and monitor the
  – quality of employee performance
  – quality control of engagements
- Using different partners and teams for the provision of non-audit services to assurance clients
- Discussing ethical issues with those charged with governance
- Consultation with another professional accountant

Individual

- Complying with continuing professional development requirements
- Keeping records of contentious issues and decisions
- Using an independent mentor
- Maintaining contact with legal advisers and professional bodies

Accountants owe their clients a **professional duty of confidence**, except in the following situations:

Obligatory disclosure

If a member knows or suspects his client to have committed a terrorist offense, an offense of **treason** or a money laundering offense he is obliged to disclose all the information at his disposal to a competent authority. In the UK, he is required to report a suspicion of money laundering. Local legislation may also require auditors to disclose other infringements.

Voluntary disclosure

In certain cases voluntary disclosure may be made by the member where:

- Disclosure is reasonable required to protect the **member's interests**
- Disclosure is required by **process of law**
- There is a **public duty** to disclose

Areas of controversy include

- Conflicts of interest
- Insider dealing

Safeguards to consider include

- Practice management issues, such as staff disclosure procedures
- Information barriers, but how successful are they?
- Engagement letters

| Fundamental principles and conceptual approach | Inde-pendence | FRC Ethical Standards | Threats | Safeguards | Confidentiality | **Conflicts of interest** | Conflicts in application of principles |

Auditors should identify potential conflicts of interest as they could result in the ethical codes being breached.

Conflicts between members' and clients' interests

Example: member competes directly with client.

———→ Do not accept engagement

Conflicts between the interests of different clients

Example: clients in competition with each other.

———→ Accept only if **safeguards** are sufficient

Safeguards include:

- **Disclosure** of the conflict to both clients
- Separate engagement teams.

2: Code of Ethics and Conduct

The general principles of the *Code* may conflict in some circumstances. This is because the *Code* is **principles-based** (not rules-based). Rather than simply following a rule, auditors must ensure they are independent by **judging how best to apply the fundamental principles**. This sometimes involves **balancing** the principles against each other. For example:

Auditor encounters a fraud	**Matters to consider where there is a conflict**
	▪ Relevant facts
Conflict: duty to report vs. confidentiality	▪ Ethical issues involved
	▪ Fundamental principles related to the matter in question
Take legal advice on whether there is duty to report	▪ Established internal procedures
	▪ Alternative courses of action

3: Professional liability

The responsibility of the auditor is simple: to report to the shareholders on the truth and fairness of the financial statements.

However, the auditor has subsidiary responsibilities and liabilities: to the company (in contract) and potentially to third party users of the financial statements (in tort).

There are some methods by which auditors may restrict their potential liability.

Auditors' responsibilities for fraud and error are a common area of public misunderstanding and an example of the expectations gap.

AUDITOR LIABILITY

Negligence

In **contract** and **tort**

A common law concept whereby a person who has suffered loss due to another persons wrongful neglect is compensated

In **criminal** law

- Various insolvency issues
- Insider dealing
- Money laundering issues

A successful claim for negligence requires:

1 An enforceable **duty of care** to have existed

2 The duty to have been **breached**

3 **Loss** to have **resulted**

Therefore, the auditor always owes the company (the client) a duty of reasonable care.

In English (and many other) law(s) a contract for service **implies** a duty of care. (In practice, this means to adhere to ISAs and other FRC guidance.)

However, such a duty of care is only **implied** to the **company**.

Various other users of financial statements (individual shareholders, employees, prospective shareholders, tax authorities, lenders, others) must seek to prove that is true in their case.

It is in the interest of the auditor to avoid liability claims.

(a) They can issue disclaimers

(b) They can make good use of **quality control** procedures to avoid problems.

(c) Client acceptance procedures are important.

If auditors are sued, they may choose to settle out of court.

Advantages
▪ Cheaper
▪ Less adverse publicity
▪ Quicker

The key case that provides insight on judicial thinking on this issue is *Caparo Industries plc v Dickman and Others 1990.*

The Caparo case

Caparo Industries purchased Fidelity shares in the open market. After the audited accounts were published they bought more and in the end, bought enough to take over Fidelity. Caparo later alleged that the audited accounts were misleading – a profit should really have been a loss. They argued the auditors owed a duty of care to investors and potential investors. The House of Lords held that **auditors did not owe a duty of care to the public at large** deciding whether to buy shares.

3: Professional liability

There are four main methods of restricting auditor liability.

Professional indemnity insurance

ACCA requirement – insurance against civil claims.

If >6 employees → must have fidelity guarantee insurance too (covers fraud by firm)

Incorporation

Auditors can incorporate in UK, and can obtained stock exchange listings.

Limited Liability Partnerships (LLPs)

Many audit firms in the UK are LLPs. This provides limited liability but with the flexibility and tax structure of a partnership.

Liability limitation agreements

Auditors have wanted limited liability agreements/liability caps for some time. This is part of the ongoing debate over the future of audit.

Fraud

An **intentional** act by one or more individuals among management, those charged with governance, employees or third parties, involving the use of deception to obtain an unjust or illegal advantage.

Respective responsibilities

The **directors** are **responsible** for preventing and detecting **fraud**.

The **auditor** is responsible **conducting an audit** in accordance with **ISAs** in order to obtain reasonable assurance that FS are free from **material misstatement** whether caused by fraud or error. Due to the limitations of audit there is still a chance of material misstatement.

Error

An **unintentional** misstatement.

Exam focus

Look for **factors** in questions which might indicate a **risk** of fraud. These could include:

- Management with poor integrity
- Deficient internal control components
- Unusual transactions
- Financial reporting pressures
- Problems in gaining sufficient appropriate evidence
- Unique issues arising from systems

3: Professional liability

Risk assessment procedures

- Inquiries of management:
    - Management's risk assessment
    - Management's process for identifying risks
    - Management's communications with those charged with governance (TCWG) regarding fraud
    - Management's communications with employees regarding best practice
    - How TCWG oversee fraud risk management
    - Whether TCWG have knowledge or suspicion of fraud/alleged fraud
- Consideration of fraud risk factors
- Consideration of results of analytical procedures
- Consideration of other relevant information

Response to risks

Overall
- Assigning appropriate staff
- Evaluation of accounting policies
- Incorporation of unpredictability

Re management override of controls
- Procedures to test:
    - Journals
    - Estimates
    - Unusual transactions

Other
- Further audit procedures as relevant

REPORTING

Reporting to those charged with governance	If the auditor suspects or detects any fraud (even if immaterial), as soon as he can he should tell: ■ The appropriate level of management (employee fraud), or ■ Those charged with governance (management fraud).
Reporting to members	In terms of the **audit opinion** given on the financial statements, if the auditor feels that the financial statements are affected by a fraud, he should **modify his report** accordingly. If the auditor feels he has to **withdraw** from the engagement as a result of his discovery, he should **consider whether** there is a professional or legal **requirement to report** to the person who appointed him.
Reporting to third parties	When the auditor discovers or suspects a fraud, he should consider whether there is a **duty to disclose**. The auditor would in practice **seek legal advice** to ensure that he was not breaching their ethical duties regarding confidentiality.

Expectations gap

Any gap between the expectations of users of audited financial statements, and those of auditors

Fraud is a common area where expectations diverge: it is sometimes incorrectly thought that the purpose of the audit is to detect fraud.

Logically, there are 2 ways of **narrowing** the gap:

Educating **users**

Eg improve audit report's explanation of audit process

Extending **auditors'** responsibilities

Eg Requiring auditors to report on the adequacy on fraud prevention controls

4: Quality control

Probably the most important consideration in practice management is quality control. This chapter covers the specific guidance in relation to quality practice and procedures: ISA 220 Quality Control for an audit of financial statements and ISQC 1 Quality Control for firms that perform audits and reviews of financial statements and other assurance and related services engagements.

ISQC 1.11

The objective of the firm is to establish and maintain a system of quality control to provide it with reasonable assurance that:
(a) The firm and its personnel comply with professional standards and applicable legal and regulatory requirements; and
(b) Reports issued by the firm or engagement partners are appropriate in the circumstances.

The entire business strategy of the firm should be driven by the need for quality.

Leadership responsibilities

- Sufficient and appropriate experience
- Ability to carry out the job
- Authority to carry out the job

Human resources

- Recruitment
- Capabilities
- Career development
- Compensation
- Performance evaluation
- Competence
- Promotion
- Estimation of personnel needs

Assignment of engagement teams

This is the responsibility of the engagement partner

Engagement performance

This involves:

- Direction
- Supervision
- Review
- Consultation
- Resolution of disputes

The firm must also have standards as to what constitutes a suitable **quality control review**

Monitoring

QC procedures must be:

- Relevant
- Adequate
- Operating effectively
- Complied with

Corrective action includes:

- Remedial action with individual
- Communication with training dept.
- Changes in QC policies and procedures
- Disciplinary action (if necessary)

ISA 220 *Quality Control for an Audit of Financial Statements* applies the general principles of ISQC 1 to individual audits.

Individual audits

- Leadership – engagement partner responsible
- Adhering to professional requirements (independence and objectivity)
- Acceptance/continuance of audit
- Appropriately qualified/experienced staff
- Engagement performance
- Monitoring QC procedures

Engagement performance

- **Direction**. Informing staff about:
  - The work to do
  - Nature of client
  - Potential problems
  - Responsibilities
- **Supervision**. Overall by engagement partner but more practical supervision given within the audit team
- **Review**. Includes consideration of whether:
  - Work complies with required standards
  - Significant matters/conclusions documented
  - Evidence is sufficient and appropriate
- **Consultation**. Contentious matters must be discussed and properly rewarded
- **Quality Control review**. Evaluation of:
  - Significant judgements
  - Conclusions

5: Obtaining and accepting professional appointments

Topic List

Change in auditor

Advertising, fees and tendering

Acceptance

Agreeing terms

Exam questions could be set in the context of a change of auditor. This could involve:

- *Ethical issues*
- *Practice management issues*

Be prepared to link issues on the syllabus when you are working through these passcards. Some questions in the exam are scenario based and bring in lots of different issues. The professional appointment may be for a service other than audit (see Chapter 12).

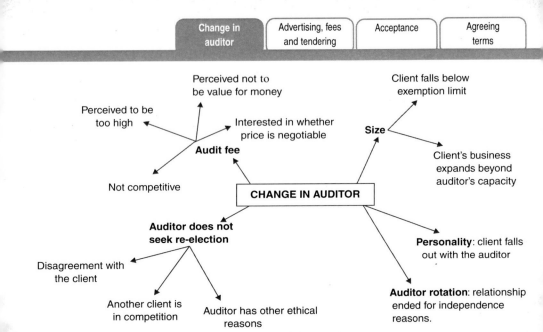

Advertising

The medium used should not reflect adversely on the member, ACCA or the accountancy profession.

Fees
■ No prescribed basis
■ %/contingency only unrelated to audit
■ Quoting too low a fee may introduce threat to competence and due care

■ Fair and reasonable re:
    – seniority of staff
    – time
    – risk/responsibility

Tendering

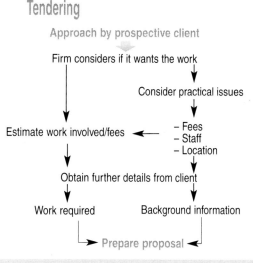

Approach by prospective client

Firm considers if it wants the work

Consider practical issues

– Fees
– Staff
– Location

Estimate work involved/fees

Obtain further details from client

Work required   Background information

Prepare proposal

ISQC 1 requires that a firm carry out the following steps when deciding whether to accept an audit:

Step 1 Obtain relevant information (eg from previous auditors, from other firm personnel)

Step 2 Identify relevant issues (eg client's integrity, firm's competence to carry out engagement)

Step 3 If resolvable issues exist, resolve them and document that resolution

Money laundering

Firms must carry out 'Know Your Client' (KYC) procedures in order to comply with Anti-Money Laundering regulations. Examples include obtaining information such as the source of the client's funds, its business model, and expected patterns of business.

Politically exposed persons (PEPs)

Being involved with PEPs may be risky for the firm – the firm must have risk management procedures to identify potential PEPs.

The auditor must be sure **preconditions for an audit** exist before agreeing terms. It is vital to agree terms with a client so that there is no misunderstanding as to what the service will be, to prevent problems later on. This is usually achieved through the **engagement letter.**

Items typically covered in an engagement letter

- The **objective/scope** of the audit (law/standards)
- **Management's responsibility** for the FS
- Identification of applicable **financial reporting framework**
- The **form** of any **reports/communications**
- **Inherent limitations** (risk of undiscovered misstatements)
- **Arrangements** regarding **planning** of the audit
- Expectations in relation to **representations**
- **Basis on** which the **fees** are computed/billing arrangements
- **Arrangements re** involvements of **IA/3P** in audit
- Any **restriction** of the **auditor's liability** where possible
- Reference to **further agreements** between client/auditor

Books/documents

Working papers are owned by the auditor. The client has no right of access to them.

UK company law is changing so that in a new audit situation, the old auditors will be required to provide access to relevant information where a new auditor makes such a request.

6: Planning and risk assessment

Topic List

Methodologies

Materiality

Risk

Analytical procedures

Planning is a key skill for an auditor. The auditor must plan the audit so as to perform it in an effective manner. Two key areas in planning are:

- *Materiality* ■ *Risk*

Exams regularly include scenarios where you need to identify either business or audit risks, so you need to have a thorough understanding of this area.

ISA 315.15

The auditor shall obtain an understanding of the entity's process for identifying business risks relevant to financial reporting objectives and deciding about actions to address those risks.

Business risk approach

(a) Recognises that most business risks will eventually have an effect on the financial statements

(b) Allows the auditor to gain a greater understanding of the business and therefore increases the chance of identifying risks of material misstatement

(c) Enables auditor to give constructive business advice

Examples of business risks → **Risks of material misstatement**

Economic pressures causing reduced unit sales and eroding margins → Inventory values (IAS 2) Going concern

Customer dissatisfaction related to inability to meet order requirements → Going concern

Economic pressures resulting in demands for extended credit → Receivables recoverability

'Top down' approach

The approach starts with the business and its objectives and works back down to the financial statements

Impact of approach on procedures

Controls testing: Auditor concentrates on more high level controls used by directors to manage risks.

Analytical procedures: Higher use than in traditional audit (consistent with desire to understand the entity).

Detailed testing: Reduced due to two factors above but not eliminated.

Advantages
■ Added value to client as business focused
■ Audit efficiency/cost is reduced
■ Focuses on corporate governance
■ Lower engagement risk as the auditor understands the client's business

Systems audit

Auditors always ascertain and evaluate the systems of an audit entity. If auditors conclude systems are:

- **Effective,** they will undertake tests of controls and aim to reduce substantive testing
- **Ineffective,** they will not test controls and undertake detailed substantive testing

Remember

Substantive testing can **never** be eliminated entirely from an audit.

Exam focus

If the auditor has adjudged that **systems** at a client are **ineffective**, he may choose the **transactions approach** to the audit so that the transactions which have gone through the **poor systems** can be **substantiated**.

Transaction cycles approach

When auditors take a cycles approach they test the **transactions** which result in the income statement. They will trace transactions through the system from order to payment.

Directional testing is an approach to testing used within a substantive approach. It is a methodology which gives assurance using the double entry accounting system.

Type of account	Purpose of primary test	Primary test also gives comfort on			
		Assets	Liabilities	Income	Expenses
Assets	Overstatement (O)	U	O	O	U
Liabilities	Understatement (U)	U	O	O	U
Income	Understatement (U)	U	O	O	U
Expenses	Overstatement (O)	U	O	O	U

The auditor will choose the audit approach which best fits the situation at the client, but may use a combination of the approaches discussed here. Therefore, directional testing can be used in a cycles or balance sheet approach, an analytical approach can be used with a business risk approach, and so on.

For you to consider

You have been asked to plan the audit of Hugues Co, a listed construction company. It has been an audit client of your firm for a number of years. You have learned the following:

The company issued a profits warning for the year three months prior to the year end. Shareholders are accustomed to receiving two dividends annually, after interim and final results are published. The company has been badly affected by the general poor economic condition in the country. Revenue on houses already built is significantly down, and advance orders on proposed new builds are also down. However, despite slow movement in house sales nationally, the company recently purchased rights to buy land in the capital city, where prices for land continues to rise.

Identify audit risks arising from the information you have been given.

(Some factors are given overleaf. You should note it is not intended to be a comprehensive answer to the question, however.)

General matters: The construction industry is subject to volatility and is therefore likely to be particularly hard hit if economic conditions are poor. Given shareholders expectations re dividends, this could lead to profit manipulation by creative accounting to give the 'best-case' picture in the accounts. The auditor may want to render materiality with regard to profit/loss quite low, particularly if the result is marginal. The issue of going concern should also be considered if sales are low, profits have been affected and if this has or will adversely affect the share price.

Inventory: The fact that revenue on already built homes is low may mean that the company has high levels of inventory, which should be investigated for obsolescence. The general increase due to poor economic conditions might hide specific and different selling problems with individual sites. Inventory affects profit.

Land: How should the transaction be accounted for? Timing of purchase: commitment or asset? Do the rights themselves have value? How have these transactions been accounted for before? Has the company entered such transactions before or is it designed to affect the accounts?

Materiality

An expression of the relative significance or importance of a particular matter in the context of the **financial statements as a whole**.

Performance materiality

The amount or amounts set by the auditor at **less than materiality for the financial statements as a whole** to reduce to an appropriately low level the probability that the aggregate of uncorrected and undetected misstatements exceeds materiality for the financial statements as a whole or **in a particular class of transaction, account balance or disclosure**.

Criteria of materiality

An item might be material due to its

Nature   eg Transactions related to directors, such as remuneration or contract with the company.
Value   eg Land with a value comprising three-quarters of a company's asset value.
Impact   eg A journal which could convert a profit into a loss.

Exam focus

In P7, calculating materiality will never get many masks by itself – it is likely to be just a starting-point for discussing issues from the **scenario**.

Rules on materiality

Materiality is judgmental, but a number of generally accepted rules do exist. An example is the range of percentage values commonly applied. When assessing materiality in exam questions calculate the relevant matter as a percentage of the relevant indicator (profit, revenue, total assets) and assess whether it falls within these ranges.

Problems with materiality

Prescriptive rules will not always be helpful when assessing materiality. There is a risk that a significant matter falls outside the boundaries of the rules and there is a material misstatement in the financial statements.

Bear in mind the focus/issues of the company being audited

assets costs
salaries profits

In order to calculate a level of planning materiality, the auditor will often take a range of values and use an average or weighted average.

Profit before tax
5%
Gross profit
1/2 – 1%
Revenue
1/2 – 1%
Total assets
1 – 2%
Net assets
2 – 5%
Profit after tax
5 – 10%

| Methodologies | Materiality | Risk | Analytical procedures |

Overview of approach

Perform risk assessment procedures (ISA 315)

↓

Assess the risk of material misstatement (ISA 315)

↓

Respond to assessed risk (ISA 330)

↓

Perform further audit procedures (ISA 330)

↓

Evaluate audit evidence obtained (ISA 330)

Audit risk

The risk that the auditor expresses an inappropriate opinion when the financial statements are materially misstated.

Inherent

- Affecting client as a whole (management integrity, nature, IT, industry factors, pressures)
- Affecting individual balances (complex accounts, assets at risk, staff)

Control

- Nature of controls
- Attitude to controls

Detection

- Chance of discovering errors

Business risk

The risk arising to a business from being in operation.

Financial

Risks arising from the financial activities or financial consequences of an operation.

Operational

Risks arising with regard to operations.

Compliance

Risk that arises from non-compliance with laws and regulations.

Examples of risks
■ Cash flow issues
■ Overtrading
■ Capital issues
■ Going concern
■ Breakdown of accounting systems
■ Credit risk
■ Loss of key supplier/customer
■ Loss of key employees
■ Physical disasters
■ Poor brand management
■ Breach of law/regulation: fines
■ Tax problems: fines
■ Environmental law: fines/compensation

Exam focus

It is vital that you do not confuse audit risk with business risk

Analytical procedures can be used in three ways during an audit:

- Risk assessment procedures
- Substantive procedures
- Overall review

Analytical procedures consist of comparing items expected to have a relationship.

In an analytical approach, this area is concentrated on more highly.

Analytical approaches are commonly taken on:

- Business risk approach assignments
- Reviews
- Assurance engagements
- Prospective financial information

Analytical approach

Is taken in situations where:

- Auditor expects little change in figures
- Auditor has high degree of knowledge of expected changes

Techniques include:

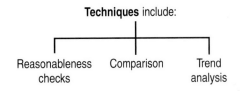

Reasonableness checks   Comparison   Trend analysis

7: Evidence

Auditors need to obtain evidence in order to reach their audit opinion. This evidence should be

- *Sufficient (a measure of quantity)*
- *Appropriate (a measure of quality)*

Some issues in FS can be difficult to obtain evidence about eg related party transactions. Transactions may not be recorded, and only management have details of who the related parties are, therefore the auditor will use management representations as evidence. Sometimes the auditor will use evidence created by third parties (internal audit or experts).

Auditors seek audit evidence about the **assertions** (the representations made by the directors in the financial statements). These are:

- **A**ccuracy
- **C**ompleteness
- **C**ut-off
- **A**llocation
- **C**lassification (understandability)
- **O**ccurrence
- **V**aluation
- **E**xistence
- **R**ights and obligations

Audit procedures

- Inspection of assets/documentation
- Observation
- Enquiry
- Confirmation
- Recalculation
- Reperformance
- Analytical procedures
- Audit automation tools

Auditors must gain sufficient, appropriate audit evidence.

Sufficient	Appropriate
■ Sampling (statistical or not) ■ Materiality ■ Risk	■ Source? ■ Oral? ■ Written?

The objectives of the auditor ... to obtain an understanding of related party relationships and transactions ... to ... recognise fraud risk factors arising ... to conclude whether the financial statements ... achieve fair presentation ...   *ISA 550*

Issues

- Inherent difficulties of (self) detection
    - Not even necessarily evident to management
    - Transactions not necessarily charged for (not processed)
    - Chance of concealment by management
    - Complex corporate structures
- Responsibility of management to identify related parties
- Materiality – adjudged in relation to related parties not entity

Evidence

There are two key problems with regard to evidence:

- May be limited
- May be created by the related party

Sources of evidence

- Minutes of meetings of those charged with governance
- Analytical review of transactions
- Confirmation of loans (eg who is guarantor)
- Written representations
- Correspondence with solicitors

The written representations of management can be a vital source of audit evidence.

The auditor needs to obtain written representations:

- About management's responsibilities/the competence of information given to the auditor
- To support other evidence when required by other ISAs or determined by auditor.

Management's responsibilities are corrected when the auditor receives a signed copy of the FS containing a statement of management's responsibilities.

Remember

Management representations cannot be used as a substitute where other evidence was expected to be available and should be available.

ISA 610 *Using the work of internal auditors* highlights three important things for the external auditor to consider when making use of the work of internal audit in the audit.

1. Understanding/assessing the role and scope of internal audit in the organisation for purposes of audit
2. Timing of liaison and co-ordination
3. Evaluating specific audit work

Steps one and two will be carried out as part of the process of **identifying and assessing the risks of material misstatement**.

If the auditors decide to make use of the work of internal audit, they must **evaluate** that work to ensure that it is **sufficient and appropriate** for them to base their opinion on. This is step three. The table adjacent gives examples of questions which they might ask.

Using the work of internal audit

- Have the internal auditors sufficient and adequate **training** to carry out the work?
- Are the internal auditors **competent**?
- Does internal audit adopt a **systematic and disciplined approach**?
- Is the work of **assistants** properly **supervised**, reviewed and documented?
- Are the **conclusions** reached **appropriate** given the evidence obtained?
- Are **reports** produced **consistent with the work** undertaken?
- Have any **unusual matters** discovered by the internal audit department been **resolved**?

Auditor's expert

is an individual or firm possessing expertise in a field other than accounting or auditing, whose work in that field is used by the auditor in obtaining, sufficient appropriate audit evidence.

ISA 620 *Using the work of an auditor's expert* identifies four issues for an auditor to assess.

1. Whether it is necessary to use an expert.

The following might require evidence from an expert:

Asset valuation, determination of quantity/ completion of assets or of specialist amounts (eg pension accounting)

2. Competence and objectivity of the expert.

The auditor must consider the professional certification of the expert, his reputation, any relationship to the entity

3. The expert's scope of work.

Agree in writing: objectives/ scope of work, general outline of matters covered, intended use of information, extent of the expert's access to information and files. Determine whether to include expert in risk discussion.

4. The actual work of the expert.

Consider: the source data used, assumptions and methods used, the timing of the work, the results in the light of the auditor's overall knowledge of the business.

8: Evaluation and review (i)

Most of this chapter is revision from your previous auditing studies. Any of them could be part of a scenario question. Alternatively, these areas could form relatively easy marks in the exam.

Overall review

Exam focus

Auditors should carry out a review of the financial statements to draw an audit conclusion (in conjunction with evidence already obtained).

- Compliance with accounting regulations/examine accounting policies
- Review for consistency and reasonableness
  - Presentation
  - Disclosure
  - New factors included

Analytical procedures

- Should be performed at end of audit.

Accounting ratios, related items, change in products/customers/price/mix/wages, impact of industry changes.

Accumulating and evaluating misstatements

The auditor must consider:

- Aggregate of known misstatements
- Whether circumstances indicate that there may be other misstatements (which are not known about)

Auditors then consider if these uncorrected misstatements are material.

All uncorrected misstatements are reported to TCWG.

Opening balances

are those account balances that exist at the beginning of the period. Opening balances are based upon the closing balances of the prior period and reflect the effects of transactions of the prior period and its accounting policies.

The auditor must obtain sufficient appropriate audit evidence that:

(a) Opening balances correctly b/f

(b) They do not contain misstatements material to current year figures

(c) Accounting policies are consistently applied or changes adequately disclosed

Incoming auditors

Testing opening balances can be difficult for new auditors because they did not audit prior year figures. They should:

(a) Ascertain whether prior report was unqualified

(b) Undertake discussions with management about opening figures

(c) Undertake substantive procedures on opening figures if concerns arise

Corresponding figures

are amounts and other disclosures for the preceding period included as part of the current period financial statements, which are intended to be read in relation to the amounts and other disclosures relating to the current period. They are distinguished from comparative financial statements, which do not form part of the current period FS, and which the auditor's report should refer to separately if they exist.

Continuing auditors

- Check balances b/f correctly
- If unresolved prior year problem is material to CY, modify report due to opening balances and comparatives
- If material to CY but opening balances are not affected, report should refer to comparatives
  - Modification
  - Emphasis of matter paragraph

Incoming auditors: audited comparatives

- Responsible for comparatives as part of CY accounts
- No reference in auditor's report
- Procedures as for continuing auditors

Incoming auditors: unaudited comparatives

- Ensure there is clear disclosure that the comparatives are unaudited
- Other Matter paragraph in auditor's report
- Should carry out procedures as for continuing auditors, as far as possible

Other information

Financial and non-financial information other than the audited financial statements and the auditor's report, which an entity may include in its annual report, either by custom or statute

Examples

- Financial summaries
- Employment data
- Financial ratios

The auditor may have responsibility to report on other information under local legislation, or may be engaged separately to do so.

  - Under UK companies legislation the auditor must state in the auditor's report whether the directors' report is consistent with the audited financial statements and whether listed companies have complied with the UK Corporate Governance Code.

On discovering a material inconsistency, the auditor should determine whether the audited financial statements or other information needs revised:

- If financial statements need revising, then modify auditor's report (ISA 705)
- If other information needs revising, include Other Matter paragraph in auditor's report

If a material misstatement of fact is discovered in the other information (but does not conflict with information in the financial statements), the auditor shall discuss this with management.

8: Evaluation and review (i)

Subsequent events

are events which occur between the period-end and the date of the auditor's report, and after.

There are two types of event (IAS 37):

- Providing evidence of conditions that existed at the period-end (**adjusting events**).

- Indicative of conditions which arose subsequent to the period-end (**non-adjusting events**).

Prior to auditor's report being signed

Auditors should carry out audit procedures designed to obtain sufficient appropriate audit evidence that subsequent events requiring adjustment or disclosure in the financial statements have been identified.

Audit procedures

- Enquiries of management

  (Status of judgmental issues, new commitments, unusual accounting adjustments, etc)

- Reading minutes of meetings

- Reviewing most recent financial information

After the auditor's report has been signed

Before FS issued

The auditor does not have any obligation to perform procedures or make enquiries regarding the financial statements after the date of his report.

If material subsequent events become known, the auditor should:

(a) Discuss the matter with management and, where appropriate, those charged with governance

(b) Consider whether the financial statements need amendment

(c) Inquire how management intends to address the matter in the financial statements

If appropriate, the auditors should extend his procedures and issue a new auditor's report.

After FS issued

The auditor has no obligation to perform procedures or make enquiries regarding the financial statements after they have been issued. When management revise the financial statements the auditor should:

(a) Carry out necessary audit procedures.

(b) Review steps taken by management to ensure anyone in receipt of the previously issued financial statements is informed.

(c) Extend the audit procedures to the date of the new auditor's report.

(d) Issue a new report on the revised financial statements.

The amended auditor's report should contain an emphasis of matter paragraph.

8: Evaluation and review (i)

Going concern assumption

An entity is ordinarily viewed as continuing in business for the foreseeable future with neither the intention nor the necessity of liquidation, ceasing trading or seeking protection from its creditors.

Auditor responsibilities

The auditor is responsible for considering the appropriateness of the going concern assumption, and the existence of any material uncertainties in relation to going concern which should be disclosed in the FS. In addition, he should consider whether the disclosures regarding the going concern basis are adequate.

Planning and risk assessment

In obtaining an understanding of the entity, the auditor should consider whether anything casts doubt on the entity's going concern status. If management have undertaken a preliminary assessment of going concern, the auditor should review it. The auditor should remain alert throughout the audit for any factors which would indicate problems (examples given below).

```
┌─────────────────────────────────────────┐
│                 Examples                  │
└──────────────────┐  ┌─────────────────────┘
                   ▼  ▼
```

Financial

- Net liabilities
- Fixed term borrowing approaching maturity without realistic prospect of renewal/repayment
- Negative operating cash flows
- Adverse financial ratios
- Substantial operation losses
- Inability to pay payables
- Inability to finance new products

Operating

- Loss of key management/markets/franchise
- Labour difficulties/supply shortage

Other

- Major legal proceedings/non-compliance

Evaluation

The auditors should consider the following when evaluating management's assessment of the entity to continue as a going concern.

(a) **Process** used by directors

(b) The **assumptions** used

(c) The **plans** for future action

Additional audit procedures

Auditors may have to carry out additional procedures when questions arise on the appropriateness of the going concern assumption. Examples include:

Analyse and discuss cash flow/profit/other forecasts/interim financial information with management, review the terms of debentures/ loan agreements, read minutes of meetings, make enquiries of lawyers regarding legal claims.

Reporting

Adequate disclosure

⬇

Emphasis of matter paragraph

Without qualifying our opinion we draw attention to Note X in the financial statements which indicates that the company incurred a net loss of ZZZ during the year ended December 31, 20X1 and, as of that date, the company's current liabilities exceeded its total assets by YYY. These conclusions, along with other matters as set forth in Note X, indicate the existence of a material uncertainty that may cast significant doubt about the company's ability to continue as a going concern.

Inadequate disclosure

⬇

Qualified/adverse opinion:

- Going concern appropriate, but material uncertainties not adequately disclosed
  → Qualifed/adverse opinion

- Going concern not appropriate → Adverse opinion

If there are multiple material uncertainties that are significant to the financial statements as a whole, the auditor may consider it appropriate to express a **disclaimer of opinion**.

9: Evaluation and review (ii) matters relating to specific accounting issues

Topic List

Fair value

Inventories and construction contracts

Tangible and intangible non-current assets

Financial instruments

Investment properties

Foreign exchange rates

In the exam you will be expected to evaluate the issues surrounding items in FS from an audit perspective. The key matters you should consider are:

- *Materiality*
- *Relevant accounting standards*
- *Risk*
- *Audit evidence to be sought*

Much of this will depend on the particular issues raised in a question. This chapter gives some pointers in terms of accounting standards/audit procedures. Remember any of the accounting areas you have previously studied could come up in this exam.

Accounting estimate

An approximation of a monetary amount in the absence of a precise means of measurement. The term is used for an amount measured at fair value where there is estimation uncertainty as well as for other amounts that require estimation.

The auditor is required to assess the entity's process for determining accounting estimates including fair value measurements and disclosures and the related control activities and to assess the arising risks of material misstatement.

Once the auditors have assessed the risks associated with determining fair value, they should design further procedures to address those risks.

IFRS 13 contains extensive guidance on measuring FVs. There is a risk that this has not been followed.

Audit procedures

- Refer to the market where FV=market value
- Use the work of an expert
- Consider management's past history of carrying out its stated intentions with respect to assets or liabilities
- Review written plans and other documentation
- Consider management's stated reasons for choosing a particular course of action
- Consider management's ability to carry out a particular course of action

Inventory (IAS 2)

Is valuation basis reasonable?

- Purchase invoices
- Price index
- Enquire

Is calculation correct?

- Check maths
- Consider if reasonable
- Verify to invoices, personnel records, nominal expense accounts
- Use analytical procedures?

Construction contracts (IAS 11)

Revenue and profit recognised must reflect the stage of contract activity at the end of the reporting period. Profit should not be taken up if uncertain, and losses should be recognised immediately.

Procedures

- Check maths of calculation
- Is basis of calculation comparable?
- Verify figures:
  - Revenue to certificate
  - Contract price to contract
  - Work completed to invoices
  - Payments to remittances
- Discuss losses arising with management

9: Evaluation and review (ii) matters relating to specific accounting issues

Tangible non-current assets

Main accounting aspects of IAS 16 *Property, plant and equipment* are assumed knowledge from earlier studies.

Key issues

Key issues likely to relate to

- Depreciation
- Disposals
- Revaluations
- Impairments

Impairments

IAS 36 *Impairment of assets* is relevant to the **valuation** assertion.

Audit procedures

- Identify any indicators of impairment
- Review calculation of recoverable amount
- Assess reasonableness of cash flows used in value in use calculation
- Consider the use of an expert to corroborate the net realisable value
- Check that any impairment losses recognised are correctly written off

Goodwill (IFRS 3)

Purchased goodwill should be capitalised as an asset. NCI is measured either at fair value, or as a proportionate share of net assets. Internally generated goodwill (including brands) should not be capitalised.

Audit tests

- Prepare analysis of movements
- Obtain any third party confirmations
- Review specialist valuations
- Inspect purchase documentation
- Confirm authorisation
- Check computation of amortisation
- Review sales returns for income

Development costs (IAS 38)

The criteria for allowing development costs to be capitalised are:

- Technically feasible
- Intention to complete/sell
- Ability to use/sell
- Existence of a market
- Availability of resources
- Expenditure can be measured reliably

Audit tests

- Check accounting records
- Review market research
- Review budgets/forecast cash
- Check amortisation

In other words, ensure that the criteria are met and disclosure is correct.

Financial instruments

Classification

- Amortised cost
- Fair value

Existence

- Examine certificates of title
- Third party confirmations
- Transfer documents
- Purchase invoices/contracts
- Sales invoices

Other aspects

- Consider **business risk** (management may not fully understand it)
- The more **complex** the financial instruments, the greater the need for **professional skepticism**

Valuation

- Utilise information from 3rd party, eg a **broker**
- Gather data and **develop own estimation model**
- **Engage an expert**
- Check basis is appropriate per IAS 32/IAS 39/ IFRS 7/ IFRS 9

Investment income

- Ensure only recognised when appropriate

Completeness/occurrence/measurement

- Check all income received
- Review for unusual entries

Investment property

is **property held to earn rentals** or for **capital appreciation**, rather than for:

(a) use in the production or supply of goods or for administrative proposals; or

(b) sale in the ordinary course of business.

Substantive tests

- Verify rental agreements
- Check architect's certificates if recently built

IAS 40

- Held initially at cost, then choice of cost or fair value model
- Disclose details of valuers and bases of valuation used
- Changes in fair value taken to profit or loss

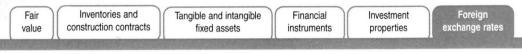

The presence of **foreign exchange** is likely to **increase audit risk**.

Individual company

Risk is that IAS 21 *The effects of changes in foreign exchange rates* is not complied with.

Audit procedures:

- Check monetary items in SOFP are translated at Closing Rate
- Check non-monetary items translated at Historical Rate
- Check SoPLOCI items translation at Historical Rate

Groups

If a parent has a different **functional currency** from its subsidiaries, then:

- Check that assets & liabilities translated at Closing Rate
- Check that income statement items translated at Historical Rate (or average rate)
- Check that exchange differences are reported in equity.

10: Evaluation and review (iii) matters relating to specific accounting issues

Topic List

Income

Liabilities

Expenses

Disclosure and other issues

In the exam you will be expected to evaluate the issues surrounding items in FS from an audit perspective. The key matters you should consider are:

- *Materiality*
- *Relevant accounting standards*
- *Risk*
- *Audit evidence to be sought*

*Much of this will depend on the particular issues raised in a question. This chapter gives some pointers in terms of accounting standards/audit procedures. Remember any of the financial reporting areas you have previously studied **could** come up in this exam.*

Revenue recognition

Accounting treatment found in IAS 18 *Revenue*. Revenue is often audited using **analytical procedures** as it has predictable relationships and there is lots of available information about it.

ISA 240 states that auditors must presume there is a **risk of fraud** in revenue recognition.

Government grants and assistance IAS 20

Revenue
- Check classification
- Agree to documentation (eg letter/application)
- Agree receipt to bank statements

Capital
- Accounting basis comparable to PY?
- Discuss with directors
- Agree any transfers between SoFP and SoPLOCI. (This should be like testing depreciation.)

Finance lease

transfers substantially all the risks and rewards of ownership of an asset to the lessee.

Sale and finance leaseback

- No sale in accordance with IAS 17
- Sale proceeds treated as finance lease liability

Operating lease

is a lease other than a finance lease.

Sale and operating leaseback

(a) If SP = FV, recognise profit/loss immediately

(b) If SP < FV, recognise profit/loss immediately unless the apparent loss is compensated by future rentals at below market price. In this case defer and amortise over remainder of lease term.

(c) If SP > FV, the profit in excess of fair value should be deferred and amortised over the period for which the asset is expected to be used.

10: Evaluation and review (iii) matters relating to specific accounting issues

Audit procedures

Classification and rights and obligations

- Obtain copy lease agreement
- Review lease agreement to ensure correct lease classification under IAS 17

Sale and leaseback

- Review terms of agreement to confirm whether finance/operating sale and leaseback
- Confirm treatment of any profit loss in accordance with IAS 17

Valuation (finance leases)

- Obtain client workings in relation to finance leases
- Check additions and calculations of workings
- Ensure interest accounted for in accordance IAS 17
- Recalculate interest
- Agree opening position
- Agree any new assets to lease agreements
- Verify lease payments in the year to the bank statements

Valuation (operating leases)

- Agree payments to bank statements (if material)

Deferred tax

This the tax attributable to timing differences. Full provision must be made for deferred tax assets and liabilities arising from timing differences between items in the financial statements and the tax computation.

Deferred tax

1. Obtain an copy of the deferred tax workings and the corporation tax computation
2. Check the arithmetical **accuracy** of the deferred tax working
3. Agree the **figures used** to calculate timing differences to those on the **tax computation** and the **financial statements**
4. Consider the assumptions made in the light of your knowledge of the business and any other evidence gathered during the course of the audit to ensure **reasonableness**
5. Agree the opening position on the deferred tax account to the prior year financial statements
6. Review the basis of the provision to ensure:
   - It is line with accounting practice under IAS 12 *Income taxes*
   - It is suitably comparable to practice in previous years
   - Any changes in accounting policy have been disclosed

Provision

This is a liability of of uncertain timing or amount, to be settled by the transfer of economic benefits.

Contingent liability

A possible obligation to be confirmed by uncertain future events not in the entity's control, or an obligation where the amount of the obligation cannot be measured with sufficient reliability.

Contingent asset

A possible asset arising from past events to be confirmed by future events not wholly within the entity's control.

Audit procedures

The auditor has to assess the treatment of provisions against the adjacent criteria.

Evidence to consider

- Reviewing correspondence
- Discussion with the directors
- Referring to comparable past events
- Seeking verification from solicitors
- Recalculating provisions for accuracy
- Considering the nature of the business

IAS 37

A provision should be recognised as a liability when **all** the following apply:

(a) An entity has a present obligation (legal or constructive) from a past event
(b) It is probable that a transfer of economic benefits will be required to settle it
(c) A reliable estimate can be made of the obligation.

Specific Guidance

- Restructuring
- Onerous contracts
- Decommissioning

Accounting estimate

is an approximation of the amount of a monetary amount in the absence of a precise means of measurement

Auditor's point estimate

the amount or range of amounts, respectively, derived from audit evidence for use in evaluating management's point estimate.

The auditor should obtain sufficient appropriate evidence regarding accounting estimates.

- Assess risks
- Evaluate risks
- Perform further audit procedures
- Assess for indicators of management bias

IFRS 2 *Share-based payment*

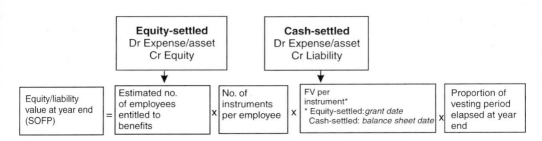

Statement of profit or loss charge = movement on SOFP.

IAS 19 *Employee benefits*

Types of plans

Defined contribution
– accruals basis
– no actuarial assumptions

Defined benefit
– more complex
– actuarial assumptions to estimate future liabilities

Statement of financial position
Liability =
PV of defined obligation at SFP date

+ Actuarial gains/- actuarial losses

– Past service cost not yet recognised

– Fair value of assets at SFP date

Statement of profit or loss
Expense = total of:
Current service cost
Interest
Expected return on any plan assets
Actuarial gains/losses
Past service cost
Effect of any curtailments/settlements

Audit procedures: pension costs

- Review actuary's report
- Assess reasonableness of assumptions
  - investment returns
  - interest rates
  - terms of scheme
- Review board minutes post year end

Segmental information

Accounting treatment found in IFRS 8 *Operating segments*

- Obtain schedule of workings
- Discuss method with directors
- Verify a sample of items to sales invoices

Discontinued operations

Accounting treatment found in IFRS 5. May be **material** through size/nature.

- Discuss with management
- Review minutes/correspondence
- Agree workings to FS
- Trace sample to invoices

Earnings per share

Accounting treatment found in IAS 33 *Earnings per share*.

Likely to be **material** because of the nature of the ratio: investor interest.

- Recalculate to check accuracy
- Ensure consistent with other years

Statements of cash flows

Accounting treatment found in IAS 7 *Statements of cash flows*.

Statement of cash flows is often audited by the auditor reproducing it from the other audited information (SoPLOCI and SoFP). However, may be checked line by line.

Borrowing costs

Accounting treatment found in IAS 23 *Borrowing costs*. Finance costs must represent the **effective interest rate** which may differ from the coupon rate paid on borrowings.

- Obtain client workings
- Review for correctness
- Agree relevant figures to FS
- Agree figures to lender statement

11: Group audits and transnational audits

When faced with a question about auditing in a group context remember that there are two aspects:

- *Single company audit issues (for the parent or subsidiaries individually)*
- *Group audit issues (discussed in this chapter).*

Group financial statements

Financial statements that include the financial information of more than one component.

Component

An entity whose financial information is included in the group financial statements.

Acceptance and continuance

MUST determine whether sufficient appropriate audit evidence can be obtained in the consolidation process and the financial information of components.

Group engagement partner

The partner who is responsible for the group audit engagement and the auditor's report on the group financial statements.

Responsibilities

- Direction, supervision and performance of group audit
- Opinion on group financial statements

NO reference to component auditors in the report.

Group engagement team

Partners and staff who establish the overall group audit strategy, communicate with component auditors, perform work on the consolidation process and evaluate the conclusions drawn from the audit evidence as the basis for forming an opinion on the group financial statements.

Component auditors

An auditor who, at the request of the group engagement team, performs work on financial information of a component for the group audit

Understanding the component auditors

Group engagement team must obtain an understanding of:

- Whether the component auditor understands the relevant ethical requirements and is independent
- The component auditor's professional competence
- Whether the group engagement team will have sufficient involvement in the work of the component auditor
- Whether the component auditor operates in a regulatory environment that actively oversees auditors

Communication with the component auditors

Engagement team will communicate:

- Work to be performed and the use to be made of it
- A request to confirm that component auditor will co-operate with the group engagement team
- Relevant ethical requirements
- Component materiality
- Identified significant risks
- Related parties

Component auditor will communicate:

- Identification of information reported on
- Risks of material misstatements in group financial statements
- Lists of uncorrected misstatements
- Indicators of management bias
- Material deficiencies in internal control over financial reporting
- Other significant matters including fraud/suspected fraud

The group engagement team shall determine the type of work to be performed on the financial information of components in response to assessed risks

Group engagement team must be involved in risk assessment

Significant components

Components that are not significant

Work to be done by group engagement team or component auditor on their behalf

Group engagement team shall perform analytical procedures at group level.

Individual financial significance

Significant due to risks of material misstatements due to specific circumstances

One of:
- (full) audit of financial information using component materiality
- audit of one or more account balances or classes of transaction relating to the likely risks
- specified audit procedures relating to the likely risks

(Full) Audit of financial information

Evaluation of component auditors work

- Evaluate communications from component auditor
- Discuss matters arising with component auditor or component management
- Decide whether it is necessary to review parts of component auditor's audit documentation
- **If** conclusion is that component auditor's work is insufficient, determine additional procedures required

Step 1   Check the **transposition** from the audited accounts of each subsidiary/associate to the consolidation schedules.

Step 2   Check that adjustments made on consolidation are appropriate and comparable with the previous year.

This will involve:

- **Recording** the **dates** and **costs of acquisitions** of subsidiaries and the assets acquired
- **Calculating goodwill** and **pre-acquisition reserves** arising on consolidation
- **Preparing** an overall **reconciliation** of movements on reserves and non-controlling interests

Step 3   Check for business acquisitions

- That combination has been **appropriately treated** as an acquisition
- Review the policy chosen re whether or not to measure NCI at FV
- The **appropriateness** of the **date** used as the date of combination
- The **treatment** of the **results** of **investments** acquired during the year
- That the **fair value** of acquired **assets** and **liabilities** is reasonable (to ascertainable market value by use of an expert)
- **Goodwill** has been **calculated correctly** and reviewed for impairment

Step 4   Check for disposals:

- The **appropriateness** of the **date** used as the date for disposal. This can be agreed to sales documentation
- Whether the **results** of the **investment** have been **included** up to the date of disposal, and whether figures used are reasonable

(Audited figures may not be available, and management accounts may have to be used.)

Step 5   **Consider** whether **previous treatment** of **existing subsidiaries** or **associates** is still **correct** (consider level of influence, degree of support)

Step 6   Verify the **arithmetical accuracy** of the consolidation workings

Step 7   **Review** the **consolidated accounts** for **compliance** with legislation, accounting standards and other relevant regulations. Care will need to be taken where:

- Group companies do not have coterminous accounting periods
- Subsidiaries are not consolidated
- Accounting policies of group members differ because foreign subsidiaries operate under different rules

Step 8   Other important areas include:

- Treatment of participating interests and associates
- Treatment of goodwill and intangible assets
- Foreign currency legislation
- Treatment of loss-making subsidiaries
- Treatment of restrictions on distribution of profits of a subsidiary

Review the **consolidated accounts** to confirm that they give a true and fair view in the circumstance

Joint audit

is one 'where two or more auditors are responsible for an audit engagement and jointly produce an audit report to the client'.

Both firms must sign the audit report and will be **jointly liable** in the event of litigation.

Reasons

- Takeover
- Locational problems
- Political problems
- Preference for local accountants

Problems

- Expensive
- May not improve audit quality

This is a **topical area** at the moment, with proposals in existence for **compulsory joint audits** of large EU companies.

Transnational audit

An audit of **financial statements** which are or may be **relied upon outside** the audited entity's **home jurisdiction** for purposes of significant lending, investment or regulatory decisions. **Includes all** listed audit clients, or **public interest entities**.

Example

Private company in UK raising debt finance in Canada

International charity taking donations through various national branches and making grants around the world

Private Internal betting company registered in BVL, which operates from Costa Rica and takes wagers by credit card on a worldwide basis via internet

Project financial statements for the construction of an electrical generation facility in Nigeria using funds loaned by the World Bank

Transnational Auditors Committee (TAC) of IFAC

Identifies audit practice issues and makes recommendations for changes to standards

Provides a forum to discuss "best practices"

Identifies members for standard-setting boards

Acts as conduit for interaction among transnational firms and international regulators

Dominance of global accounting firms

The Big Four firms supply audit services to most large companies. The FRC and former DTI commissioned a study which identified the following potential problems.

(a) A company may have no effective choice of auditor if firms are ineligible due to independence rules.

(b) If one of the Big Four left the market, a few large companies would be unable to find an auditor.

(c) Restriction of choice may represent a risk to high quality and competitive prices.

In July 2011 the OFT referred the audit market to the competition commission, which has the power to break up firms if it sees fit to do so.

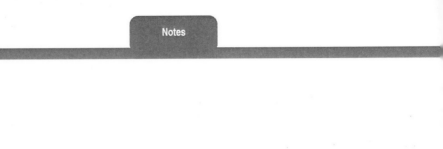

Notes

12: Audit-related services and other assurance services

The title of the paper is advanced audit and assurance, so assurance services are clearly important and you should not neglect them. Remember that the key aspect of an assurance service is that the accountant evaluates specified criteria. Audit-related services are other assignments which an auditor can undertake which are not audits.

Audit firms may be engaged to perform a variety of engagement types other than the statutory audit.

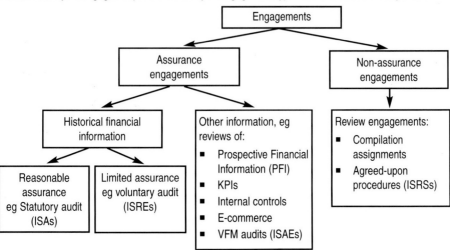

Review engagement

Enables an auditor to state whether, on the basis of procedures which do not provide all the evidence that would be required in an audit, anything has come to the auditors' attention that causes the auditor to believe that the financial statements are not prepared in accordance with the reporting framework.

Reviews follow a similar process to auditing

1. Planning
2. Seeking evidence (often analytical procedures are used)
3. Reporting conclusions

Limited assurance is given on review assignments

The review conclusion is phrased using a **negative form of words**.

Although the level of assurance is **lower** than audit, the **conclusion** may be modified in the same kinds of way:

- Qualified opinion (material, not pervasive)
- Adverse opinion (material and pervasive misstatement)
- Disclaimer of conclusion (material and pervasive inability to obtain sufficient and appropriate evidence

Agreed-upon procedures are when an auditor is engaged to carry out procedures of an audit nature which have been pre-agreed, and to report factual findings. Results confined to those parties who have commissioned the report.

If an accountant is engaged to use accounting expertise, as opposed to auditing expertise, to collect, classify and collate information, eg tax return or accounts, then this is known as **compilation engagement**.

Audit-related services

- Agree terms with relevant parties

- Carry out the agreed procedures

- Report:
    - No assurance expressed
    - Report factual findings

- Information does not have to be financial

- Information compiled should have reference to the fact that the information is unaudited

- Report: No assurance expressed

- Identification of information compiled

Take a moment or two to think of examples of assurance services, perhaps ones you have been involved in, but this doesn't have to be the case if you do not work in an assurance department. Think through the following issues in relation to each of the assurance services you have come up with:

- How does it display the criteria of a assurance service?
- For whose benefit is it carried out?
- Does it raise any issues of audit firm liability that should be thought about?
- What other issues would an auditor consider before accepting such an engagement?

These are the kind of issues you night have to think through in an exam answer.

12: Audit-related services and other assurance services

Assurance engagement

Where an accountant evaluates or measures a subject matter that is the responsibility of another party against suitable criteria, and expresses an opinion which provides the intended user with a level of assurance about that subject matter.

Accepting appointment

- Ethics/Quality Control
- Competent?
- True assurance engagement?
- Agree terms

Why

- Improves quality of decision-making for users
- Decline in audit for small companies
- Importance of computer systems

Planning

- Strategy/plan
- Professional scepticism
- Understanding of the entity/environment
- Criteria suitable?
- Materiality/risk

Assurance given

A reasonable level of assurance is given as the accountant is evaluating specific criteria. Absolute assurance can not be given.

Evidence
■ Gain appropriate evidence
■ Document matters arising
■ Consider subsequent events
■ Assess experts used

Not assurance engagements
■ Agreed upon procedures
■ Compilations
■ Tax return preparation
■ Management/tax consulting
■ Other advisory services

Reporting
■ Express conclusion giving reasonable/limited level of assurance
■ Describe criteria
■ State if restricted purpose
■ Clearly state qualifications or limitations

Responsibility

It is part of the governance duties of the directors (sometimes using internal audit) to assess and manage business risks.

Assessing risks

These risks could include, for example:

- Contractual risks (important customers not agreeing to given contractual terms)
- Operational risks (scare raw materials, risks arising through storage and use)
- Physical risks (for example, health and safety compliance)
- Product distribution (logistics, networks, outlets)
- Regulation (different jurisdictions, internet trading)
- Reputation (brands and staff profile)

Responses to risk

Management can choose to:

- Avoid risk
- Reduce risk
- Accept risk
- Transfer risk

The key way to mitigate risk is to create controls to prevent risk arising, ie the system of **internal controls** in the business.

Assurance services

- Directors' risk assessment
- Design of control system
- Operation of control system

13: Prospective financial information and insolvency

The key issues for auditors when asked to report on PFI are:

- *What their potential liability might be, and to whom*
- *The nature of the assumptions in the PFI (is it possible to draw valid conclusions?)*

Once you have understood that there are two main types of liquidation (compulsory and voluntary) and two types of voluntary liquidation (members' and creditors') it should be straightforward to learn the features of each of them.

Company administration is also important in this syllabus.

Forecast

PFI prepared on the basis of assumptions about expected future events and management actions ('best-estimate').

Projection

PFI prepared on the basis of:

- Hypothetical assumptions
- Mixture of best estimate and hypothetical assumptions ('what-if')

Key areas

- Capital expenditure
- Profits
- Cashflows

Firms are often engaged to report on PFI for various reasons. ISAE 3400 gives direction in this area. Problems include inherent uncertainties, and the extent to which auditors can be liable.

ISAE 3400

The auditor should not accept/withdraw from an engagement where the assumptions are clearly unrealistic or when the auditor believes the PFI will be inappropriate for its intended use.

The auditor and the client should agree on the terms of the engagement.

Factors to consider

- Intended **use** of the information

- Intended **distribution** of the information (limited/public)

- **Nature of the assumptions** made in the PFI (hypothetical/known/best estimate)

- **Elements** to be included in the information

- **Period** covered by the PFI (6 months ... 10 years?)

- **Knowledge** of the business (sufficient?)

- Assurance on **figures** or **conclusions** drawn by management?

There are four general matters which the auditor should review.

Business: nature/background

- Is the forecast consistent with the business?
- Is forecasting ordinary or extra-ordinary?
- Current activities/products/customers

Accounting policies used in past

- What are the accounting policies used?
- Are forecast policies consistent with normal accounting?

Assumptions forecast based on

- Are they
  - Best estimate?
  - Hypothetical?
  - Reliable?
  - Reasonable?

Procedure followed

- Backing documentation (is there any?)
- Basis
- Is the basis justified?
- Is the basis approved?

Profit forecasts

- Verify **income** figures to evidence (such as income from current projects/market prices)
- Verify **expenditure** figures to evidence (quotes/estimates/current bills/market prices)

Capital expenditure

Check cap ex projections for **reasonableness:**

- Costs verified to quotations/estimates where possible
- Other reasonableness such as prevailing market price (eg for property)

Cash forecasts

- Ensure that **timings** involved are **reasonable**
- Check that cash forecast is **consistent** with other forecasts (profit/cap ex)
- Where no other forecasts exist, check income/expenditure as outlined above

It is clear that the subjectivity of PFI means that it is impossible to give the same level of assurance in relation to PFI as for HFI (historic financial information). It is extremely difficult for auditors to report on whether forecasts are achievable. The ISAE recommends giving **negative assurance.**

An important point to remember is that responsibility for the PFI rests with management.

Negative assurance

Assurance of something in the absence of any evidence to the contrary.

ISAE 3400

ISAE 3400 recommends negative assurance that

- Assumptions are reasonable basis for PFI
- PFI is properly prepared (assumptions/framework)

The report should also include **caveats** as to the achievability of the forecasts.

Liquidation

A company is dissolved and its affairs wound up (hence it is sometimes referred to as winding up). The assets are realised, debts are paid from the proceeds and any surplus amounts are paid to members.

There are two main types of liquidation (compulsory and voluntary) which will be looked at below. When a company is liquidated, a **liquidator** must be appointed.

A liquidator must be an authorised insolvency practitioner. They have a **statutory duty** to report directors of an **insolvent company** if they are considered unfit to be involved in management.

BUT

A company does not have to be insolvent to be liquidated.

Once a company enters liquidation procedures:

- No share dealings
- Communications must state the company is in liquidation
- Director's power to manage ceases

13: Prospective financial information and insolvency

Compulsory liquidation

Various parties may apply to the court for a company to be wound up. Key reasons:

- Company is **unable to pay its debts** (creditors)
- It is **just and equitable** to wind up the company (members)
- A public limited company has traded without a **trading certificate** > 1 year
- It is in the **public interest** to wind up the company

Company cannot pay debts

A creditor can show a company is unable to pay its debts in three situations:

- A written demand is served for £750 at the registered office and the debt is still unpaid within 21 days
- There are no assets against which to enforce payment
- The creditor proves to the court that the company is unable to pay its debts.

When the court approves the order:

- Official receiver is the liquidator
- Liquidation from date petition presented
- Subsequent sale of assets void
- Legal proceedings halted
- Employees dismissed
- Floating charges crystallise

The liquidation is deemed to have started when the order was first applied for. The official receiver holds **meetings** with the creditors and contributories (members) who can appoint their own liquidator. Creditors' choice takes priority. The official receiver **must investigate the affairs** of the company and may report to the court, seeking a public examination of those responsible. They may apply to the Registrar for early dissolution if assets do not cover their expenses.

Members' voluntary liquidation

The company is solvent but the members decide to liquidate anyway.

Mostly commonly achieved by passing a **special resolution** (75%).

Directors must issue a **declaration of solvency** that debts can be paid up in full in a period < 12 months.

Creditors play no part in a members' winding up, as it is assumed the debts will be paid in full.

Creditors' voluntary liquidation

The company is insolvent and the members agree to wind it up.

Special resolution passed (75%).

Meeting of creditors convened to resolve to wind up, appoint a liquidator and nominate 5 representatives to form a liquidation committee.

If the creditors do not appoint a liquidator, the members should.

Making a declaration of solvency without reasonable grounds is a criminal offence.

Control	Compulsory liquidations are controlled by the court, members' voluntary liquidations are controlled by the members and creditors control a creditors' voluntary winding up.
Timing	A voluntary winding up commences on the day the resolution to wind up is passed. It is not retrospective. A compulsory winding up commences on the day the petition was presented to the court.
Liquidator	The official receiver plays no role in a voluntary winding up. The members or creditors select the liquidator who is not an court officer.
Legal proceedings	There is no automatic stay of legal proceedings against the company nor are previous dispositions or seizure of its assets void in a voluntary winding up. However the liquidator has a general right to apply to the court to make any order which the court can make in a compulsory liquidation.
Management and staff	In any liquidation the liquidator replaces the directors in the management of the company (unless they decide to retain them). The employees are not automatically dismissed by the commencement of voluntary liquidation. However, insolvent liquidation may amount to repudiation of their contracts of employment (and provisions of the statutory employment protection code apply).

Administration puts an insolvency practitioner in control of the company with a defined programme for rescuing it from insolvency, as a going concern (it cannot already be in liquidation). The administrator will seek to save the company, **or** to achieve a better result for creditors than immediate liquidation, **or** to realise property for distribution to creditors.

Effect of administration	Advantages of an administration
<ul><li>A moratorium commences (no creditors may enforce debts against the company)</li><li>Items with charges may be sold (fixed chargeholders to give permission)</li><li>The powers of management are subjugated to the appointed administrator, who must act in the interests of all creditors</li><li>Outstanding petitions for the winding up of the company are dismissed</li></ul>	☑ The company is not dissolved ☑ It provides breathing space to attempt a rescue of the company ☑ Past transactions of the company can be challenged ☑ It allows creditors to continue to trade with the company if the rescue is successful ☑ Members continue to own shares in the company which may be successful in the future.

The court may be petitioned for an administration order by:

- The company (a 50% majority of members) ■ The directors ■ Creditors ■ The Magistrates' Court (for non-payment of fines) NOT by individual members.

13: Prospective financial information and insolvency

Appointment of administrators without reference to the court

Certain parties can appoint an administrator without going to court.

Floating chargeholders	Company/directors
May appoint an administrator if: ■ They have given 2 days' notice to holders of prior floating charges (unless they consent) ■ The floating charge is enforceable After 2 days' notice, an appointing floating chargeholder must file certain documents at the court making the appointment valid.	May (depending on articles) appoint if: ■ No administration/moratorium in last 12 months ■ Company cannot pay debts ■ No petitions for winding up/administration have been made ■ No liquidator/administrative receiver/administrator already in office The company/directors must give floating chargeholders notice so that they may block appointment if they wish. They then file the appropriate documents with the court to make the appointment valid.

Administrator's duties

As soon as reasonably practicable after their appointment, they must send notice of it to:

- The company

- Each creditor

- The Registrar (within 7 days)

They must also **publish** news of the appointment.

They must ensure all company documents publicise that it is 'in administration'.

They must consider the **statements of affairs** submitted to them and set out proposals to achieve the aims of administration.

Administrator's proposals

- Must set out proposals to achieve the aim of liquidation OR why they do not consider it reasonable or practical that the company be rescued

- Must not affect the right of a secured creditor to enforce their security, or result in preferential debt losing priority to non-preferential debt, or to one preferential debt being paid proportionately less than another

- Must be provided if requested by the administrator. It is in a prescribed form and contains details of company property, debts and liabilities, company creditors and security given for debts.

Administrator's powers

To do anything necessarily expedient for the management of the affairs, business and property of the company:

- Remove/appoint directors
- Call meeting of creditors/members
- Apply to the court for direction
- Make payments to secured/preferential creditors
- Make payments to unsecured creditors (with court permission)

End of administration

When:

- Administration has been successful
- 12 months have passed since appointment
- The administrator or a creditor applies to court to end the appointment
- An improper motive of the applicant for applying for administration is discovered

Interaction with other insolvency procedures

- Prevents voluntary winding up application and order for compulsory winding up
- Prevents appointment of administrative receivers

The administrator must call a meeting of creditors within 10 weeks of appointment to approve the proposals.

14: Forensic audits

Forensic audit is an expanding area of work for many firms. Its applications range from fraud investigations to insurance claims.

In the pilot paper it appeared in a practical case study question and the requirements asked for practical procedures that would be applied in a specific fraud investigation.

Forensic audit

Gathering, analysing and reporting on data, for the purpose of finding facts and/or evidence in the context of financial/legal disputes and/or irregularities and giving preventative advice in this area.

Forensic investigation

Carried out for civil or criminal cases. These can involve fraud, asset tracing for money laundering.

Forensic accounting

Undertaking a financial investigation in response to a particular event, where the findings may be used as evidence in court or to help resolve disputes.

Main applications	Other disputes
■ Fraud investigations	■ Shareholder
■ Negligence cases	■ Partnership disputes
■ Insurance claims	■ Contract disputes
■ Terrorist financing	■ Sales and purchase disputes
■ Expert witness	■ Matrimonial disputes

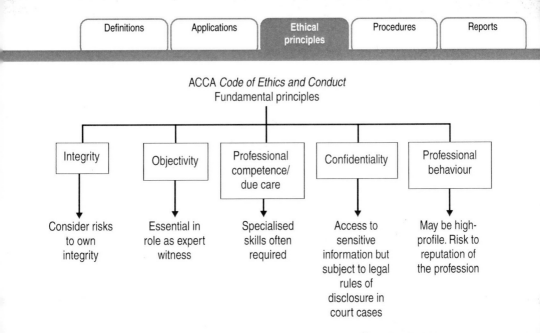

| Definitions | Applications | **Ethical principles** | Procedures | Reports |

ACCA *Code of Ethics and Conduct*
Fundamental principles

| Integrity | Objectivity | Professional competence/ due care | Confidentiality | Professional behaviour |

Consider risks to own integrity

Essential in role as expert witness

Specialised skills often required

Access to sensitive information but subject to legal rules of disclosure in court cases

May be high-profile. Risk to reputation of the profession

The procedures used in forensic work are likely to be very similar to those used in other types of audit and assurance assignment.

Key considerations

- Materiality – likely to be **no materiality** threshold

- Timing – needs to be **unpredictable**

- Documentation – reviewed **more critically** than for audit

- Interviewing – aim to obtain **admission**

- Computer-aided techniques – may employ techniques such as **data-mining**

Reports

Expert witness reports

Key elements:

- CV of expert

- Instructions and issues

- Documentation

- Chronology – factual evidence

- Opinion with explicit reasons

Other reports

Form and content of report will depend on the terms of the assignment. The principles as outlined in Chapter 17 will apply.

15: Social and environmental auditing

Topic List

Stakeholders and implications for management

Measuring social and environmental performance

Implications for the statutory audit

Implications for assurance services

Remember the implications environmental and social issues can have on the statutory audit. This could be examined in a planning scenario question. It can also be examined in the context of a company setting social and environmental performance indicators.

Shareholders   Directors   Creditors

The company

The environment

Primary impact – processes of business. Regulated by law.

Secondary impact – products. Regulated by law/consumer opinion

> Turnbull report stated that directors were responsible for risk assessment and mitigation as part of corporate governance.

Society

Society is made up of consumers.

Many make 'green' aware purchases.

May speak on behalf of the environment

Employees

Rely on the company for livelihood and safety at work.

Also form part of society, ie are potential consumers.

Risks
■ Bad publicity
■ Illegal products
■ Health and safety
■ Employee protection

Controls
■ ISO14001
■ Employment policies
■ H and S policy

Case Study

Social and environmental issues are important to Shell for various reasons: use of earth's natural resources, environmental legislation, employees working in risky environments, varied approach to human rights worldwide.

In response to these issues, the company have set social and environmental targets of performance and a set of general sustainability principles.

Social

- Zero work related employee deaths
- Not exploit child labour
- Pursue equal opportunities

Environmental

- Reduce CO_2 emissions
- Develop cleaner fuels
- Reduce all emissions
- Eliminate spills

Sustainability principles

- Respect and safeguard people
- Minimise impact on environment
- Maximise profitability
- Engage/work with stakeholders
- Use resources efficiently
- Maximise benefits to the community

The company **reports** on all these issues to its shareholders, and, wherever possible this is **verified** by independent verifiers

Social audits

A social audit is undertaken to see if social targets have been met.

Social audits

- Is there a rationale for engaging in socially responsible activities?
- Are social programmes congruent with the mission of the company?
- Assess objectives of social policies
- Evaluate the performance of the company

Environmental audits

Environmental audits seek to assess how well the organisation performs in safeguarding the environment in which it operates, and whether the company complies with environmental policies.

Audit procedures

- Obtain a copy of the environmental policy
- Assess whether it will achieve objectives
    - What are the objectives?
- Test implementation and adherence
    - Discussion
    - Observation
    - Walkthrough tests

Planning

- Knowledge of the business (ISA 315)
- Inherent risk assessment (ISA 315 and 330)

Review

- Particularly the impact on going concern (ISA 570)

Substantive procedures

- Provisions (site restoration/fines/compensation)
- Contingent liabilities (pending legal action)
- Asset values (impairment)
- Capital/revenue expenditure (clean up/rectification)
- Development costs (new products)
- Going concern issues

Audit procedure pointers

- Use minutes of meetings/correspondence
- Review trade magazines/newspapers
- Discuss with management

Types of services

- Internal audit (risks/controls)
- Review of internal controls
- Management letter (byproduct of audit)
- Independent verification assurance services

Remember

An assurance engagement is where an accountant evaluates a subject matter which is the responsibility of another party against suitable criteria and expresses an opinion to give the user a level of assurance.

Case Study (continued)

The directors in the case study could make assertions such as:

- CO_2 emissions were X million tonnes in 2001, a 2% decrease from 2000
- We have implemented a strategy to ensure that in 5 years, no one we deal with will have involvement with child labour

These assertions can be reviewed and assurance given about them. The contents of an assurance report could include the objectives, opinions, basis of the opinions, the work performance, and any limitations.

16: Internal audit and outsourcing

Both the topics in this chapter could form part of a question on audit planning. An external auditor would need to consider the implications for this audit of the client having an internal audit department, or outsourcing some of its functions.

Alternatively, either subject could be examined as an essay style question. Internal audit could feature as part of a question on corporate governance and the responsibilities of directors.

Corporate governance

Turnbull guidelines relating to:

- Internal controls
- Managing risks
- Monitoring

Internal auditors have a role in assisting directors, particularly with regard to internal controls and monitoring.

Internal auditors and risk management

In response to the Turnbull guidance, directors need to take three steps in their business:

1. Identify risks
2. Control risks
3. Monitor risks

Use by external auditors

Consider the following:

- Proficiency/training of staff
- Supervision/documentation/review
- Sufficient/appropriate evidence
- Appropriateness of conclusions
- Consistency of reports
- Amendments to our programme?

1 Identify risks

A detailed review of the following systems will be required:

- Information flow
- Document trail

This is an area of expertise for internal auditors.

2 Control risks

The methods will depend on the risks. Broad measures include:

- Training/communication
- Risk awareness at all levels

Risk policies

- Accept risk (low impact/likelihood)
- Reduce risk (set up IC system)
- Avoid risk (don't accept contract etc)
- Transfer risk (take out insurance)

3 Monitor risks

The entire process needs to be monitored to ensure that the process is followed continuously. Internal auditors are well placed to monitor. Alternatively this could be an external assurance service.

Potential risks	
■ Contractual risks	■ Product distribution
■ Operational risks	■ Regulation
■ Physical risks	■ Reputation

Operational audits

Operational audits are audits of the operational processes of the organisation and check not only compliance with controls but also the effectiveness of the controls.

Compliance audits

Compliance audits are audit checks intended to determine whether employee actions are in accordance with policy/law/regulations.

Multi-site operations

Approaches:

- Compliance approach
    - Cyclical
    - Risk based

- Process based approach
    - Cyclical
    - Risk based

Practical considerations:

- Where to go/how often/when
- Routine/surprise visits
- Size of operations
- History of systems compliance
- Management interest

Outsourcing

This is the process of purchasing key functions from an outside supplier – contracting out certain functions. **Insourcing**, is when an organisation decides to retain a centralised department for the key function, but brings experts in from an external market on a short-term basis to account for "peak" and "trough" periods.

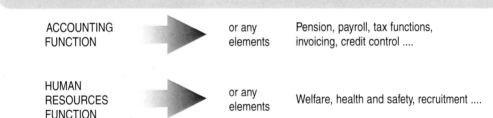

| ACCOUNTING FUNCTION | | or any elements | Pension, payroll, tax functions, invoicing, credit control .... |
| HUMAN RESOURCES FUNCTION | | or any elements | Welfare, health and safety, recruitment .... |

16: Internal audit and outsourcing

Advantages to client

Cost. It is often cheaper to contract a service out than it is to conduct it in house.

Specialist service. Specialists are used to provide the service.

Indemnity. The service organisation may provide indemnity in the event of problems arising.

Cash flow. It may assist with cash flow, as the contract will represent a flat fee. The cost of providing the service in house might have led to fluctuating costs.

Disadvantages to client

The company loses **control** over function to an extent.

The **initial cost** of outsourcing may be **substantial**, if an aspect of the decision is to close a current department of the business, for example, **potential redundancies.**

The contract has to be **managed** to ensure that the service being provided is appropriate and in accordance with the contract. This may take a disproportionate amount of **time.**

The contract might limit the **liability** of the contractor, leading to problems if the contract is not performed well. This might even result in **court action** being required.

The above could cause the **cost** of outsourcing to outweigh the benefit.

Problems with internal audit

- Cost of recruiting staff

- Need for staff of particular skill/qualification

- Difficulty of managing an internal audit department for directors

- Extended time frame between set up and results

- Work involved may not justify a full time team

- Team might be required due to variety of skill needed

Advantages of outsourcing

- Service provider has good quality staff

- Has specialist skill

- Can direct their own work and educate management as to the service required

- Provides immediate team

- Can be appointed for appropriate timescale

- Is likely to cost less than setting up a department

Data processing	*Disadvantages*	There may be **logistical difficulties** in outsourcing data processing, due to the high level of paper involved (invoices, goods received notes etc). This information will have to be given to the service organisation.
	Advantages	A secondary, and more important, effect is that the company might not always have control of their key accounting documentation and records. It is a **legal requirement** that the directors maintain this information. While they may delegate the practicalities, they are still responsible for maintaining the records.
Pensions	*Advantages*	Pensions are a specialist area and there is merit in getting a specialist to operate the company's pension provision.
	Disadvantages	Pensions are closely related to the payroll and the company will need to share sensitive information with the pension provider, which may make the situation complicated.
Due diligence	*Advantages*	A key advantage in relation to outsourcing due diligence is the high level of **expertise** that can be brought in.
		The company can expect **quality** from its service contractor, and can seek **legal compensation** from them in the event of negligence.

Information technology	Advantages	A key advantage of outsourcing all, or elements of, the IT function is that this will enable the company to keep pace with rapid **technological advances**.
		It also allows the company to take advantage of the work of specialist in a field that many people still find difficult but which they use regularly to carry out their business.
		Outsourcing can provide a useful safety net of a technical helpline or indemnity in the event of computer disaster.
		It is also possible that through outsourcing, the company will be able to obtain added-value, such as new ways of doing business identified (for example, e-commerce).
Taxes	Advantages	In relation to taxes, the key advantage is also the buying in of **expertise**.
	Disadvantages	The disadvantage of outsourcing tax work is that while the work can be outsourced, the **responsibility** cannot. The tax authorities will deal with the responsible person, not the agent, so the loss of control is particularly risky in this case.

Service organisation

This is an organisation that provides services to another organisation. A user entity is the entity which purchases those services.

Planning

- Know what is outsourced
- Understand the contract
- Risk of misstatement

Designing procedures

Depends on
- Contract nature
- Degree of authority delegated
- Quality assurance
- Nature of assets involved
- Reputation of service provider

Auditor considerations with regard to the contract

- Are the terms of the contract with the service organisation sufficiently clear for the service to be good?
- How are the relevant accounting records maintained?
- Does the user entity have the right to inspect the service organisation's records?
- Do the terms of the agreement take account of any relevant regulatory requirements?
- Does the user entity monitor the performance?
- Does the service organisation indemnify the user?
- Can the auditors have access to relevant records?

Procedures	
■ Inspecting records and documents held by the user entity	■ Requesting specified procedures re performed by
	– The service organisation
■ Establishing the effectiveness of internal control	– The user entity's internal audit department
■ Obtaining representations to confirm balance and transactions from the service organisation	■ Reviewing information from the service organisation or its auditors concerning the design and operation of its control systems
■ Performing analytical review on	
– The records maintained by the user entity, or	
– The returns received from the service organisation	

Using reports

If the auditor makes use of the service organisation's report, he should consider the reputation/skill of the service provider, and what the report is about. He must not refer to the report in his audit report.

17: Reporting

The impact of certain items on the auditor's report is examined regularly. You should work through this chapter in conjunction with Chapters 9 and 10, always bearing in mind the impact of accounting treatments and materiality on the auditor's report.

You could be asked to judge the 'effectiveness' of the auditor's report in a short a scenario about auditor's reports. You need to be able to decide on the type of report that is needed, and must be able to criticise 'draft' auditor's reports. You will need to think practically about what the auditor should do in a given situation.

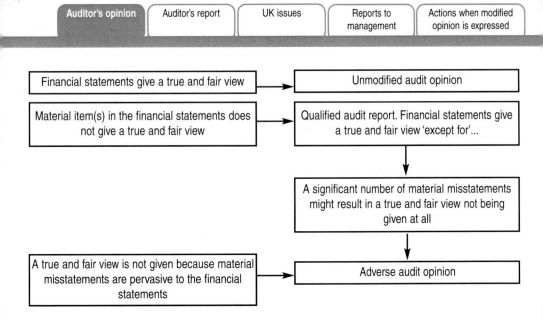

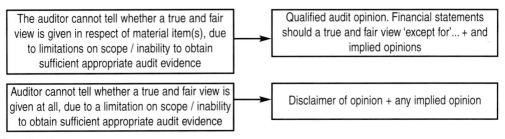

The auditor cannot tell whether a true and fair view is given in respect of material item(s), due to limitations on scope / inability to obtain sufficient appropriate audit evidence → Qualified audit opinion. Financial statements should a true and fair view 'except for'... + and implied opinions

Auditor cannot tell whether a true and fair view is given at all, due to a limitation on scope / inability to obtain sufficient appropriate audit evidence → Disclaimer of opinion + any implied opinion

Question 1

Have all the procedures necessary to meet auditing standards and to obtain all the information and explanations necessary for the audit have been carried out?

Question 2

Have the financial statements been prepared in accordance with the applicable accounting requirements?

Question 3

Do the financial statements give a true and fair view?

The process of forming an audit opinion can be summarised in a step format, as follows:

Step 1 Read through all the information given in the question carefully and analyse the requirement.

Step 2 Read through the information given in the question again in the light of the requirement, making notes of any key factors.

Step 3 Ascertain whether all the evidence reasonably expected to be available has been obtained and evaluated.

Step 4 If not, identify whether the effect of not gaining evidence is such that the financial statements could as a whole be misleading (disclaimer of opinion) or in material part could be misleading ('except for' opinion).

Step 5 Ascertain whether the financial statements have been prepared in accordance with IFRSs

Step 6 If not, determine whether departure was required to give a true and fair view and if so, whether it has been properly disclosed.

Step 7 Decide whether any unnecessary departure is material to the financial statements ('except for' opinion) or is pervasive to them (adverse opinion).

Step 8 Conclude whether the financial statements as a whole give a true and fair view.

Even if the answers to steps 3 and 5 are yes, you must still carry out step 8 and make an overall assessment of the truth and fairness of the financial statements in order to conclude that an unmodified opinion is appropriate.

You should be aware of the various modifications to an auditor's opinion (qualified adverse, disclaimer) from your pervious studies.

Critically appraising an auditor's opinion

This will involve the reviewer forming his own opinion and then comparing it to the original to see if he feels the original opinion is reasonable.

Why?
■ Engagement partner reviewing the file
■ Auditor asked for second opinion
■ 'Peer' or 'hot' review

THE STEP PROCESS JUST DISCUSSED IS THEREFORE VITAL FOR YOUR EXAM

Exam focus

You are extremely likely to be examined on this skill. You must practice the questions on this area in the Practice and Revision Kit.

So is knowing what the standard report should look like in case a report you have been asked to critique is presented wrongly.

Independent Auditor's Report to the Members of XYZ PLC

We have audited the financial statements of (name of company) for the year ended ... which comprise [specify the titles of the primary statements such as the Statement of Financial Position, the Statement of Profit or Loss and other Comprehensive Income, the Statement of Cash Flows, the Statement of Changes in Equity] and the related notes. The financial reporting framework that has been applied in their preparation is applicable law and International Financial Reporting Standards (IFRSs) as adopted by the European Union.

Respective responsibilities of directors and auditor

As explained more fully in the Directors' Responsibilities Statement [set out [on page ...]], the directors are responsible for the preparation of the financial statements and for being satisfied that they give a true and fair view. Our responsibility is to audit and express an opinion on the financial statements in accordance with applicable law and International Standards on Auditing UK and Ireland). Those standards require us to comply with the Auditing Practices Board's [(APB's)] Ethical Standards for Auditors.

Scope of the audit of the financial statements

An audit involves obtaining evidence about the amounts and disclosures in the financial statements sufficient to give reasonable assurance that the financial statements are free from material misstatement, whether caused by fraud or error. This includes an assessment of: whether the accounting policies are appropriate to the company's circumstances and have been consistently applied and adequately disclosed; the reasonableness of significant accounting estimates made by the directors; and the overall presentation of the financial statements. In addition, we read all the financial and non-financial information in the [describe the annual report] to identify material inconsistencies with the audited financial statements and to identify any information that is apparently materially incorrect based on, or materially inconsistent with, the knowledge acquired by us in the course of performing the audit. If we become aware of any apparent material misstatements or inconsistencies we consider the implications for our report.

Opinion on financial statements

In our opinion the financial statements

- give a true and fair view of the state of the company's affairs as at .... and of its profit [loss] for the year then ended;
- have been properly prepared in accordance with IFRSs as adopted by the European Union; and
- have been prepared in accordance with the requirements of the Companies Act 2006 and Article 4 of IAS Regulation.

Our assessment of risks of material misstatement

[Insert a description of those specific assessed risks of material misstatement that wereidentified by the auditor and which had the greatest effect on the audit strategy; the allocation ofresources in the audit; and directing the efforts of the engagement team.]

Our application of materiality

[Insert an explanation of how the auditor applied the concept of materiality in planning andperforming the audit. Such explanation shall specify the threshold used by the auditor as beingmateriality for the financial statements as a whole.]

An overview of the scope of our audit

[Insert an overview of the scope of the audit, including an explanation of how the scopeaddressed the assessed risks of material misstatement and was influenced by the auditor'sapplication of materiality.]

Opinion on other matters prescribed by the Companies Act 2006

In our opinion:

- the part of the Directors' Remuneration Report to be audited has been properly prepared in accordance with the Companies Act 2006; and
- the information given in the Directors' Report for the financial year for which the financial statements are prepared is consistent with the financial statements.

Matter on which we are required to report by exception

We have nothing to report in respect of the following:

Under the ISAs (UK and Ireland), we are required to report to you if, in our opinion, informationin the annual report is:

- materially inconsistent with the information in the audited financial statements; or
- apparently materially incorrect based on, or materially inconsistent with, ourknowledge of the Group acquired in the course of performing our audit; or
- is otherwise misleading.

In particular, we are required to consider whether we have identified any inconsistenciesbetween our knowledge acquired during the audit and the directors' statement that theyconsider the annual report is fair, balanced and understandable and whether the annual reportappropriately discloses those matters that we communicated to the audit committee which weconsider should have been disclosed.

Under the Companies Act 2006 we are required to report to you if, in our opinion:

- adequate accounting records have not been kept, or returns adequate for our audit have not been received from branches not visited by us; or
- the financial statements and the part of the Directors' Remuneration Report to be audited are not in agreement with the accounting records and returns; or
- certain disclosures of directors' remuneration specified by law are not made; or
- we have not received all the information and explanations we require for our audit.

[Signature]	*Address*
John Smith (Senior statutory auditor)	*Date*
for and on behalf of ABC LLP, Statutory Auditor	

Merits of the report	Criticism of the report

• The report clearly spells out **to whom** the report is **addressed**
• The report clearly states the **financial statements** it refers to
• The report refers to the **respective responsibilities** of directors/auditors
• It outlines the **process** of auditing
• It explains the audit opinion
	• Steps taken are insufficient and the report is **not clear** to a non-financial investor
	• The report includes incomprehensible **audit jargon**
	  – True and fair
	  – Materiality
	• Description of audit **unclear**
	• Extent of management responsibility not clear

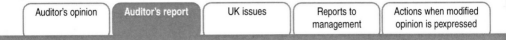

| Auditor's opinion | Auditor's report | UK issues | Reports to management | Actions when modified opinion is pexpressed |

Emphasis of matter paragraph

An EoM paragraph **does not modify the auditor's opinion** – it modifies the report. An EoM is used where the auditor wishes to draw attention to a matter that is not materially misstated in the FS.

Examples include:

- where there is significant uncertainty over going concern which FS disclose adequately
- where there is a significant uncertainty over the recovery of a material receivables balance.

Other matter paragraph

An Other Matter paragraph is used to draw attention to something other than the FS being audited.

Examples include:

- Where prior period FS were not audited at all
- Where other information must be revised, eg because it is inconsistent with the FS and the FS are not materially misstated.

Signature

Audit reports must now bear the name of the individual auditor or, in the case of a firm of auditors being used, the senior statutory auditor in his own name. Previously auditor's reports were signed in the name of the firm.

Summary financial statements

The auditors must state whether the SFS are **consistent** with the actual accounts, and **comply** with law and standards

CA 2006 includes provisions dealing with accounts found to be defective after being laid.

Offences in connection with the auditor's report

CA 2006 has introduced a new offence of 'knowingly or recklessly' causing an auditor's report to include any matter that is misleading, false or deceptive in a material particular.

Listed companies

Auditors of listed companies are required by the Listing Rules to review:

- the directors' statement on going concern
- statements of compliance with the UK CG Code
- parts of the Board's report on director's remuneration

Reporting to those charged with governance

Guidance on reporting to management and other non-shareholders as a by-product of audit is given in ISA 260 *Communication of audit matters with those charged with governance.*

Governance

Is the term used to describe the role of persons entrusted with the supervision, control and direction of the entity. Those charged with governance ordinarily are accountable for ensuring that the entity achieves its objectives, financial reporting and reporting to interested parties. Those charged with governance include management only when it performs such functions.

Matters should be discussed with those charged with governance on a **sufficiently prompt basis** that they can react to what the auditor has said. The auditor should determine whom those charged with governance are.

If an **audit committee** exists, it is likely to be the appropriate body to report matters arising from the audit to.

Communications to audit committee

- General approach and overall scope
- Selection of, or changes in, significant accounting policies
- The potential effect on the FS of any material risks, and exposures, eg pending litigation, that are required to be disclosed in the account
- Findings from the audit and their impact on the audit report
- Unadjusted misstatements, and the reasons for them
- Significant matters arising, for example, law and regulations, fraud and error, internal control issues
- Material uncertainties affecting the organisation's ability to continue as a going concern
- Significant disagreements with management
- Other matters mentioned in terms of engagement

When the auditor expresses a modified opinion, simply issuing the auditor's report is not the end of the story.

Actions when modified opinion expressed

Communicate with TCWG

- Communicate all surrounding circumstances

- Allows TCWG to provide more information before report issued

- Applies to EoM & OM as well

- Communicate other 'significant difficulties'

External consultation

Consult with:

- Legal counsel (confidentially)

- ACCA (anonymously)

Management integrity?

Especially if scope of audit is limited.

- Reconsider if representations are reliable

- Possibly perform 'hot' review

Withdrawal from engagement

Only if matter is *very* serious.

- Consult with legal counsel

If limitation on proir your audit means disclaimer of opinion this year, do not accept engagement

18: Current issues

Current issues may feature within questions on a range of topics in this exam. It is important that you keep up to date with topical issues within the audit and assurance profession. Keep a look out for relevant articles in Student Accountant.

Auditor's reports

There has been extensive debate over possible improvements to the auditor's report.

The IAASB has suggested an extensive "Auditor Commentary" for public interest entities. This would highlight the matters the auditor considers most important to users' understanding of the financial statements.

Some respondents expressed concerns that this would extend auditors' responsibilities too far, and that this is the proper responsibility of management.

Notes

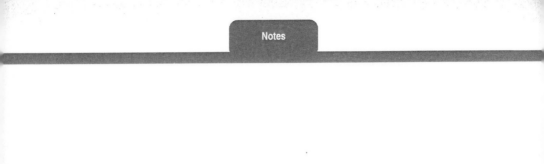

Notes